~ P O S T C A R D S   F R O M  ~

GW00392984

ROCK FER....
NEW FERRY & BEBINGTON

Dave Mitchelson

SIGMA Leisure

First published in 1989 as "Rock Ferry, New Ferry & Bebington: a portrait in photographs and old picture postcards" by S.B. Publications

This fully revised edition is published by Sigma Leisure – an imprint of Sigma Press, 1 South Oak Lane, Wilmslow, Cheshire SK9 6AR, England.

British Library Cataloguing in Publication Data
A CIP record for this book is available from the British Library.

ISBN: 1-85058-666-7

Typesetting and Design by: Sigma Press, Wilmslow, Cheshire.

Cover photograph: Entrance to Rock Ferry Pier, Bedford Road, c. 1903

CONTENTS

Page

Foreword by Jack and Bill Fairs
Introduction
Greetings from Rock Ferry.. 1 – 2
Aerial view of Rock Ferry.. 3
The Royal Rock Hotel.. 4
The Olympian Gardens 5
Bedford Road and Ferry Entrance.. 6 – 7
The Esplanade .... 8 – 9
Rock Ferry Pier... 10 – 11
The Training Ships.. 12 – 15
Rock Park... 16 – 19
St. Peter's Road.. 20 – 21
"The Barn Chapel".. 22
New Chester Road .... 23 – 26
Mersey Road School 27
Bedford Road 28
Ionic Road School 29
Bedford Road .... 30 – 32
Grove Road 33
Highfield Road.. 34 – 35
Rock Lane West 36
Highfield South, The Cinder Path.. 37
Victoria Drive, Herman House.. 38 – 39
H.M.S. Conway, R.U.F.C. 40
Charlie Broad 41
Dacre Hill .... 42 – 43
Egerton Park .... 44 – 45
St. Paul's Church 46

CONTENTS CONTINUED

	Page
Dacre Hill	47
Kings Lane	48 – 50
A "Vulgar" Postcard	51
The Dell, New Ferry	52 – 53
The Gap and Pier, New Ferry	54 – 57
New Ferry Road	58
New Ferry Shore	59
The Great Eastern	60
New Ferry Brickworks	61
The Clarence	62
The Open Air Baths, New Ferry	63
New Chester Road	64 – 66
Bebington Road, New Ferry	67
Townfield Lane, Bebington	68
The Village, Bebington	69 – 73
The Curious Inscriptions	74
Bebington Road	75 – 77
The New Drill Hall, Bebington	78
Lower Bebington School	79
Kirket Lane, Bebington	80
Mill Road, Higher Bebington	81
Storeton Woods and Quarries	82 – 86
Brackenwood House	87
Raby Mere	88
Dibbinsdale	89
Spital Park	90

Acknowledgements
S. B. Publications

FOREWORD

by Jack and Bill Fairs

We were born in Rock Ferry and have known Dave Mitchelson for many years. Consequently, we are delighted to write the foreword to his first book. To our knowledge, this is the first publication we have seen illustrating the area's history with early photographs and postcards. It gives a peep into the early part of this century, showing a fascinating glimpse of familiar landmarks and streets which have altered so much over the years.

There must be many older folk today who can remember the Storeton Quarries in operation, and the thrilling sight of the 'Conway' anchored in the River Mersey. We ourselves can remember paying only a halfpenny for a tram ride from St. Paul's Road to attend Cammel Laird's Sea Scouts.

We think this book is a splendid idea and sincerely hope that this will be the first of many books that Dave will produce.

THE AUTHOR

Dave Mitchelson (1937 - 1994) was born in Rock Ferry, where he lived for all his life.

For almost forty years, Dave was a supporter of nature conservation. For a number of years, he was a Park Ranger for Wirral Borough Council and was a leader and guide on local history walks. His special interests were butterflies and wild flowers and, over the years, he built up a large photographic library on these subjects. In more recent years, he also amassed a large collection of slides and photographs of local history and became a founder member of the Wirral Postcard Club. He used his extensive photographic library in illustrated talks.

Dave Mitchelson also compiled *Postcards from the Past: Old Bebington*, which was republished in 1998 by Sigma Leisure.

INTRODUCTION

For some time now I have wanted to write the story of Rock Ferry - the place where I was born and consequently grew to love. So, Rock Ferry - where did it all start and who started it?

The area we now know as Rock Ferry was once in the ownership of one Robert De Bebynton - as early as the reign of Edward 1. It later descended to the Mynshull family who owned the land for several generations. The ancient seat of the Mynshulls was Derby House and, as far as is known, their surrounding land extended from Old Chester Road to the shores of the River Mersey. In those days it must have been wonderful to observe, at first hand, the development of the port of Liverpool - without the screening presence of buildings that exists today. Upon the marriage of heiress Elizabeth Mynshull to Thomas Cholmondeley of Cheshire during the early part of the seventeenth century, the land changed hands again. It remained in the Cholmondeley family for three generations and was subsequently sold piecemeal by Charles Cholmondeley in the mid-eighteenth century. Derby House - or at least the last Derby House - stood on the corner of Rock Lane West and New Chester Road but was pulled down in 1929 when it was owned by the Oakshott family. The Melville Housing Estate now stands on the site.

Before being named Rock Ferry, the area was known as Bebington Inferior. It is believed that a ferry service was in existence as early as 1709, but of this there is no documentary proof. By 1790, New Chester Road had reached Rock Ferry and the ferry was in the hands of a Mr. White of Sutton who obtained an act for the improvement of the ferry in 1805. In 1820, Thomas Morecroft acquired the ferry and built the slipway. By this time Rock Ferry proved to be one of the most important ferries in Cheshire. Sometime in 1836, the Royal Rock Ferry Company was formed and took over the running of the ferry. I like to believe that this heralded the start of Rock Ferry. Unfortunately, from being one of the most sort-after residential areas in Wirral, the town has declined to what it is today. What the future holds I shudder to think!

I believe that postcards and old photographs are a record of history, people and places, and that they should be preserved in private collections or public libraries where future generations can see where and how their ancestors lived. In the following pages I have tried to record some of the memories of the people and places in Rock Ferry.

Dave Mitchelson
March 1989

ROCK FERRY, c. 1924

The "multiview" was a very popular type of postcard as it provided the sender with a more complete picture of a holiday visit to send home.

Clockwise, from the top left, this card has views of: New Chester Road, with the Palace Picture House; The Ferry; H.M.S. 'Conway'; Bedford Avenue; Bedford Road; Rock Park and, in the centre, a view of the 'Mauritania' anchored in the Mersey.

I'm Thinking
of You at
ROCK FERRY

As closely as the ivy green
My thoughts will cling to thee
And I'll be happy all the while,
If you sometimes think of me.

"THINKING OF YOU AT ROCK FERRY", c. 1903

Today, it is hard to believe that Rock Ferry once had beautiful cards like this one printed for its visitors. However, an extract from Slaters Directory of Cheshire for 1869 states: "Rock Ferry is a beautiful suburb and contains many elegant houses and villas, the residences of gentry and Liverpool merchants. Along the riverside from here to New Ferry is a good esplanade, a favourite promenade for both inhabitants and visitors".

This postcard is what is known as a stock card, one that was published for general use and overprinted with the name of the town in which it would be sold.

AERIAL VIEW OF ROCK FERRY, c. 1924

The large building in the centre of the photograph is the Royal Rock Hotel, with the Olympian Gardens to its rear. St. Margaret's Convent can be seen in the top left. Bath Cottages are facing on to the Esplanade in the left foreground. The road is Bedford Road which runs down to the Pier and to the right of it, the building with the curved frontage is the Admiral public house, with Bond's Boat Yard next door. The path running past the yard was a continuation of the Esplanade and went as far as St. Paul's Road.

Royal Rock Hotel, Rock Ferry, Birkenhead. Family and Commercial Hotel

THE ROYAL ROCK HOTEL, c. 1906

The original building was erected on this site about 1805. In 1836 the hotel and pleasure gardens were extended. It is understood that the title "Royal" was conferred by King George IV who resided here whilst visiting friends. The district has a previous royal association as the children of George III were sent here because the air was so good! The Hotel was demolished in the 1960s, at the time of the construction of the Rock Ferry bypass. A sad end to a wonderful place that had given pleasure to so many.

THE OLYMPIAN GARDENS, c. 1912

Situated at the rear of the Royal Rock Hotel, the Gardens had a separate entrance on Bedford Road. In 1910, variety shows were started here by Mr. Charles Boult and gave a great deal of pleasure to people of Rock Ferry and Liverpool who came in droves each weekend. Even boys from the 'Conway' and 'Indefatigable' training ships were regular visitors. There was one show nightly, admittance was 4d., with a folding chair 9d., whilst 1/3d. bought a seat in a deck chair on the front row. Several stars began their careers here including Douglas Furber, Stanley Holloway, Dan Leno and Little Tich.

The picture shows "The Sunbeams", a pierrot troupe from New Brighton - note their dummy propped up against a tree. The shows ceased in 1925 when Charles Boult died and the Olympian Gardens closed.

THE ROCK TAP, BEDFORD ROAD, c. 1913

Looking down Bedford Road towards the Ferry entrance with the Rock Tap or Rock Vaults on the right-hand side. It stood between the Royal Rock Hotel and the entrance to the Olympian Gardens and was extensively used by local fishermen and ferry passengers. According to local hearsay it was also used by the poorer people of the area. At the time, a typical weekly wage was between 10/- and 15/- (50p and 75p) and beer was 2$\frac{1}{2}$d. per pint and tobacco 3d. an ounce.

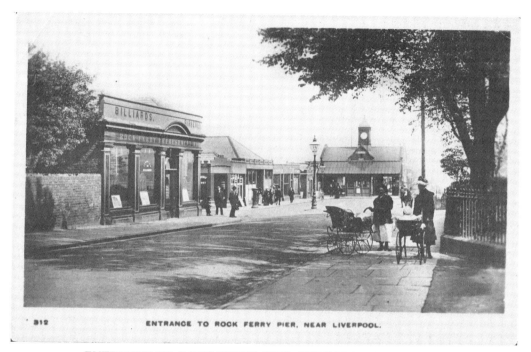

ENTRANCE TO ROCK FERRY PIER, NEAR LIVERPOOL.

ENTRANCE TO ROCK FERRY PIER, BEDFORD ROAD, c. 1903

On the left-hand side are the Rock Ferry Refreshment Rooms where gentlemen could partake of a game of billiards whilst ladies could be served high tea. This building later became Donovan's public house, now know as the Admiral. Next door to the tea rooms is the Liverpool Echo Office to which the newspapers were delivered by ferry for onward distribution to local newsagents. Beyond, another shop sold postcards and souvenirs. On the right of the photograph, behind the tree, is the entrance to the Esplanade where the ladies had just been walking with their prams.

THE ESPLANADE, c. 1913
Built in 1836, this promenade was a regular haunt for courting couples, pierrots,
photographers and three-wheel "stop-me-and-buy-ones". It was from this point that it
was once possible to take donkey rides along the golden sands to New Ferry.
New Ferry Pier can be seen in the distance.

BATH COTTAGES, THE ESPLANADE, c. 1906
Originally, the cottages were a single building providing hot and cold baths for residents and visitors. The date of construction is not known, but the building is shown on the Rock Park Estate deeds of 1837 and was in use when the Royal Rock Ferry Co., formed in 1836, took over the running of the ferry. The original plan consisted of a central keeper's facility with a row of bathrooms off both side corridors. Sometime after 1896 the building was converted into separate dwellings. Today, the cottages are part of the Rock Park Conservation Area and are the oldest buildings in Rock Park and the only ones to face directly onto the Esplanade.

Rock Ferry Pier.

The Wrench Series, No. 7565

ROCK FERRY PIER, c. 1907

The slipway was built by Thomas Morecroft in 1820 so that passengers could board the ferries. In 1836, the Royal Rock Ferry Co. took over and ran the service after making improvements. By 1897 the ferry was in the hands of Birkenhead Corporation. Due to a lack of passengers, the service closed in 1939 when, on June 14th, the ferry-boat 'Upton' carried many passengers and local dignitaries on the last trip to Liverpool. The ferry office was later used by Sea Cadets and then briefly housed the Tranmere Sailing Club but, when it became unsafe, it was pulled down. The slipway is one of Rock Ferry's oldest structures and still stands today.

ROCK FERRY PIER, c. 1902
This view is looking back towards the ferry office from the 780ft-long pier.
On the left, behind the trees, is the Royal Rock Hotel and, on the right, a turret of
Victorian construction used as a flagstaff.

THE 'CONWAY', c. 1919

The 'Conway' was moored off Rock Ferry on February 14th, 1859. An extract from the Liverpool Mercury of that year states, "To the attraction of that tempting resort Rock Ferry there has been added the frigate 'Conway' training school". By 1861, the ship was too small for the number of cadets on board. In 1862, the 'Winchester', a sixty-gun frigate built in 1822, was renamed 'Conway', moored off Rock Ferry and by June, had 107 cadets on board. In 1877, a larger ship was required again. H.M.S. 'Nile' was commissioned and, in August, renamed 'Conway' and moored off Rock Ferry. She was in the Mersey until 1941 when, because of the war, she was towed to Bangor where she remained until 1953. Sadly, while under tow for a refit she snapped her towing line, drifted onto rocks and broke her back.

THE 'AKBAR', c. 1900

The first reformatory ship to be moored off Rock Ferry was the 'Cornwallis', renamed 'Akbar' in 1811. Built in 1801 as a thirty-eight gun frigate, she was bought by the Royal Navy and from 1834 served as a quarantine ship for the port of Liverpool. 'Akbar' was in position by 1856 and made ready to accommodate 200 boys. Her role was to take Protestant offenders, aged from 12 to 15, for corrective training. Punishment for escapees was a flogging with a birch rod and 3 days bread and water. This first ship lasted 6 years and was replaced by H.M.S. 'Hero', renamed Akbar. She remained here until 1907 when she was towed away for dismantling. During her 50 years as a reformatory over 3,000 boys walked her decks. The school became a shore-based ship at Heswall, now known as Liverpool Boys Club.

13

THE INDEFATIGABLE, — RIVER MERSEY.   ART SERIES. D.

THE 'INDEFATIGABLE', c. 1903
Commonly known as the "Indie", this old wooden wall was built in 1848 and moored off
Rock Ferry by 1864. She was originally moored close to the 'Conway' but was later
moved to a position off New Ferry where she remained until 1914. Her role was to cater
for orphans and children of "poor circumstance". In 1914, she was replaced by a metal
ship which lasted until 1941.

THE "MAGNIFICENT THREE", c. 1906
This photograph was taken from the end of Rock Ferry Pier by Mr. George Davies, a well-known local photographer. It shows the three training ships in the early morning light. From left to right they are the 'Conway', 'Akbar' and 'Indefatigable'. What a wonderful sight these ships would have been to walkers, ferry passengers and, sometimes to royalty as Rock Ferry was frequently visited by the Royal Family.

ENTRANCE TO ROCK PARK, c. 1910

A design for the estate was drawn up in 1837 by Jonathan Benson. It was to be in an informal landscape setting in the romantic tradition. By 1850, the houses were completed and showed a diversity of style characteristic of the period. The stone-built houses on the water-front were amongst the earliest to be built and the stucco semi-detached blocks were amongst the latest. The Park was originally enclosed and the houses were approached from the gateway shown on this postcard. The toll lodge can just be seen to the right of the gates.

ROCK PARK, THE TOLL-COTTAGE, c. 1962

The small toll-cottage, built in Gothic style, was where tolls were collected from those using the Park. The interior consisted of a living room with kitchen area, and two small bedrooms. The keeper had a small plot at the side and rear of the building, where he grew his own vegetables and kept several hives of bees. The cottage was demolished in the late 1960s and it seems that there was no need for this senseless destruction as the land is unused today. At the time of the picture, the tolls levied were: bicycles 1d., motor cycles 3d., light cars 4d. and heavy vehicles 6d.

ROCK FERRY PARK   55561. JV.

INSIDE ROCK PARK, c. 1907

The Park is in a delightful setting on the banks of the Mersey and has a curved drive, as seen on the postcard. Nathaniel Hawthorne, the author, lived at No. 26 whilst serving as an American Consul in Liverpool. He described the Park as follows: "At the gates there is a little Gothic structure where the collection of tolls precludes all un-necessary passage of carriages, and never were there more noiseless streets than those that give access to these pretty residences. On either side there is a big shrubbery with glimpses through ornamental portals or into trim gardens with smooth shaven lawns".

INSIDE ROCK PARK, c. 1902

The estate remained more or less unchanged until the mid 1960s, when some of the houses were demolished to make way for the Rock Ferry bypass. Most of the remaining houses are Grade 2-listed buildings and are regarded as being of special historical and architectural interest. They are now included in the Conservation Area, as are the remains of the Barton Estate and part of the Dell. The New Ferry and Rock Ferry Conservation Society was formed in 1980 to protect the environment and promote the interests of people living in the area.

CAMMEL LAIRD SPORTS FIELD, ST. PETER'S ROAD, c. 1914
The ground stood on the corner of St. Peter's Road and Delta Road and the facilities available were football, cricket, bowls and tennis. The photograph shows the cricket square and pavilion. The groundsman for many years was Mr. Albert Jackson. Unfortunately, the coming of the Rock Ferry bypass put an end to the sporting activities at Cammel Laird's. In the background, the large house on the left was Kirklands, and the church spire is St. Peter's.

ST. PETER'S CHURCH, ROCK FERRY.   'The Unique Series'.

ST. PETER'S CHURCH, c. 1909

This fine old church is situated in St. Peter's Road, off Rock Lane East. The foundation stone was laid in April 1841. The church is built of red stone from Runcorn, supplied by a Mr. Tomkinson, at a cost of 5½d. per foot. Built to accommodate 756 people, the total cost of the church was £2,387. It was opened for divine service on September 8th, 1842 by the Rev. Chancellor Raikes, and consecrated on June 4th, 1844.

The Rev. T. F. Redhead was the first vicar of the parish. In 1941, both the church and vicarage were badly damaged by bombs and rendered unsafe. A year later, parishioners cleared some two tons of masonry so that a centenary service could be held. Happily, the building was renovated after World War 2 and is still in use today.

"THE BARN CHAPEL"

The oldest, but least known, church of Rock Ferry was a type of "barn chapel" which once stood on or near Rock Lane East. The writer, Knowle S. Jones, in his book "The St. Peter's Centenary, 1844 to 1944" says: "as to the precise location of the chapel it is impossible to obtain any definite information, but it is believed that it once stood at the rear of the Abbotsford Hotel on a site once occupied by Botts Dairy".

Although no pictures of the chapel are known, it probably looked like the one in the above sketch, without the headstones.

411   NEW CHESTER ROAD, ROCK FERRY.

NEW CHESTER ROAD, c. 1919

This postcard shows the crossroads at Rock Lane East and Rock Lane West. At the beginning of this century, there were many fine hotels in Rock Ferry and the large building on the right of this picture was one of the finest. It was built in the late 1870s and had its own grounds and stables. The grounds were well-maintained with a profusion of flowering shrubs and mature trees, and the surrounding walls were draped with ivy. Unfortunately, the hotel was bombed during World War 2 and was consequently demolished. The Abbotsford public house now stands in its place.

NEW CHESTER ROAD, c. 1922

On the left is the corner of Rock Lane West and from here to Bedford Road in the distance, New Chester Road was full of high-class shops. According to the author's mother, they sold only top quality goods. The corner shop was Henderson's millinery, where one could purchase silk hats embellished with ostrich feathers. Next door was Sam Garner's milk shop, later Miss Millington's. Sam was often seen in Rock Ferry, pulling his milk churn on wheels. You could buy a pennyworth of milk from him, or by taking your own jug, it would be filled for 2d. In the centre of the picture a tram makes its way to New Ferry, and in the distance is the spire of the Presbyterian church.

Rock Ferry.   New Chester Road.

The Wrench Series, No. 7568

"THE PRESBYTERIAN", NEW CHESTER ROAD, c. 1906

This was the only name that the church was known by. It was built in 1858 with seating for 600 people and stood on New Chester Road, midway between Rock Lane and Bedford Road. The spire was removed sometime in the 1950s and the remainder of the building was pulled down in early 1987. On the opposite side of the road is a building that was erected in the 1880s. It was used as a skating-rink before it became a Salvation Army barracks. The premises were next used by the parish of St. Peter's and the considerable sum of £2,000 was spent on the conversion to a parish hall. In 1911, the building was sold to a syndicate for £2,000 and became the Palace Picture House. In the foreground a single-decker tram is on its way to Woodside. The other vehicles are horse-drawn.

THE PALACE PICTURE HOUSE, NEW CHESTER ROAD, c. 1913

Taken a few years later, this photograph shows the old parish hall after its conversion to the Palace Picture House. Notice the decorative facade. The Palace was one of the first cinemas to obtain a licence to open on Sundays. This was shortly after World War 2 and the author can remember the church community marching up and down outside the Palace, waving placards condemning people for going to a cinema on Sundays! Films were shown until the 1960s when the building was sold again and converted to the present car show-room - Palace Motors. The row of houses beyond was known as Georges View.

MERSEY ROAD SCHOOL, c. 1900

This school, which was officially called Rock Ferry Higher Grade School, was one of, if not the first school in Rock Ferry. The cost of sending a child there was 7d. per week (about 3p). With the opening of Ionic Street, the Dell and Alpha Drive Schools, the Mersey Road School was forced to close in 1934. During and after World War 2, the building was used as a factory for canning vegetables. The site is now covered by the Rock Ferry bypass.

Bedford Rd, Rock Ferry.

BEDFORD ROAD, c. 1907

This postcard shows the junction at New Chester Road and the hustle and bustle that was once Bedford Road - with shops galore lining both sides of the road. The Midland Bank, which still stands today, can be clearly seen on the left of the picture. On the opposite corner is Butcher's Family Boot and Shoe Shop with large posters announcing "a great clearaway sale - Extraordinary Bargains!". Policemen on point duty were a common sight on most major crossings, where they could easily be called in an emergency. This was often necessary here as large numbers of cattle were frequently herded along New Chester Road to the abattoir in Birkenhead.

IONIC STREET SCHOOL, c. 1916
The school was built in 1913 to accommodate 910 mixed junior and infant pupils. It was taken over by the Armed Forces in about 1915, and partly used as a military hospital - the lower classrooms being used as wards. The blackboards can be seen on the wall behind the nurses. The message on the card reads, "Dear Antie Lill this is my school the army go there now Sue". The school is still in use today.

BEDFORD ROAD, c. 1906

Another busy scene in Bedford Road with the taxis lining up on both sides of the street, waiting for rail passengers who would be driven to their destinations all over Rock Ferry. The station is just to the left of the picture and not on the photograph. The Bedford Hotel is prominent on the left-hand side with its sign advertising Allsop's and Birkenhead Brewery Ales. Just beyond is a laundry, and further down the road, towards New Chester Road, many small shops appear to be doing a brisk trade. Note the two young boys in the road - the one on the left has bare feet. Behind the taxis on the right, just out of the photograph, was Holding's Coal Office. Their motto was "Lang may ya lum reek" - long may your chimney smoke!

Rock Ferry.   Station.

The Wrench Series, No. 7570

ROCK FERRY STATION, c. 1910

The station was built in 1846 to serve Rock Ferry on the Birkenhead to Chester line
which had been completed in 1840. In January 1886, the Mersey rail tunnel was
completed and was opened by the Prince of Wales. Completion of the electric line
from Liverpool to Rock Ferry, some two years later, made access to Liverpool and
Birkenhead more convenient for local people. The lines to Wallasey, Hoylake and West
Kirby were opened about the same time, and Rock Ferry became a busy railway
junction. Passengers travelling between Liverpool and Chester would change trains
here - from the electric to the steam railway. The postcard shows an early electric train.

BEDFORD ROAD, c. 1905

This photograph shows a view looking towards the Bedford Hotel, with the station in the distance. The row of taxis on the hill are parked in the same spot as those on the postcard on page 30. Behind the high wall on the right, St. Anne's Convent once stood. It was pulled down in the late 1970s to make way for a modern housing complex for the elderly. The photograph was taken on a sunny day and the awnings are down over the shops. Two sailors are walking towards the cameraman - perhaps they were 'Conway' boys.

GROVE ROAD, c. 1903

This has always been - and still is - a busy part of Rock Ferry. There are houses on one side of the road and shops on the other. Sometime in the 1920s, the ivy-covered house was converted into a fish and chip shop owned by Mr. Willcocks. At the far end of the road, the Globe Theatre once stood. It was run by Stanley and Mabel Russell.
The author's mother appeared in a few shows at this theatre; one that she remembered well was "The Fairs of Lily Vale", performed in 1913.

ST. ANNE'S ROMAN CATHOLIC CHURCH, c. 1911
This impressive church stands in Highfield Road and was built in 1887, with seating for 600 people. For many years it was not possible to see the beauty of the building because of a high surrounding wall and adjacent nunnery - both of which have now gone. In their place, some very pleasant residences for the elderly have been built. Next to the church is the priest's house and a social club. A school used to exist at the rear of the church, but the building is now used as a community centre.

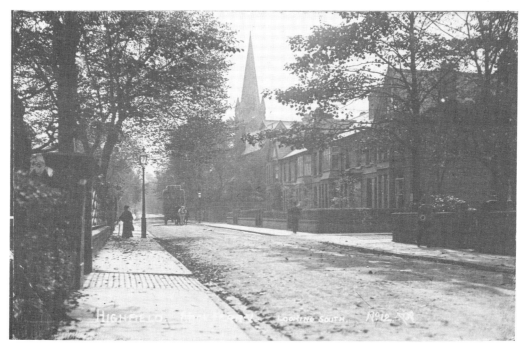

HIGHFIELD ROAD, c. 1910

This road runs from Rock Lane West to Bedford Road and this view is looking south
towards Rock Lane West. The church in the background is Highfield Congregational
Church, built in 1870 with seating for 814 people. The road on the right is Browning
Avenue, and to the south of the church is Highfield South - at one time a cul-de-sac
leading to two houses only. In the centre of the road, two shire horses are hauling a
large load of hay bales whilst the farmhand walks alongside; this would not have been
an uncommon sight in Rock Ferry at the beginning of the century.

35

ROCK LANE WEST, c. 1914

In the 1870s, Rock Lane West consisted of just four or five large villas and a church which stood on the corner of Highfield South - the road on the right of the postcard. The lane was used extensively by stage-coaches transporting passengers and mail to "far off" places such as Neston and Parkgate. By the 1900s, it had been totally transformed from a country lane to a high-class residential area with houses on both sides of the road, most of which had their own stables and outdoor and domestic staff. A large house near the top of the lane was taken over by the G.P.O. in the 1940s and turned into a telephone exchange. The transformation was total and not a sign of the house remains today.

THE CINDER PATH, HIGHFIELD SOUTH, c. 1913

This footpath, locally known as the "Cinder Path", is 346 yards long and runs from halfway along Highfield South to Old Chester Road at Woodhey. It originally carried on to Higher Bebington along what is now Town Lane. To the right of the path, the grounds, part of the Crowe family home, were unique in that they contained a wide variety of trees of different species. In 1925, the house was taken over by Birkenhead Council for use as a High School to accommodate 360 boys. It now forms part of Rock Ferry High Comprehensive School. Some local people are posing for the cameraman, Mr. George Davies. The boy leaning against the railings is wearing the uniform of a telegraph boy.

HERMAN HOUSE, VICTORIA DRIVE, c. 1905

Herman House or, to give it its proper name, Tinwald, stands on the corner of Rock Lane West and Victoria Drive. It was built in the 1880s and converted to a school, "Misses Ladies School", which opened in 1886. In 1896, an advertisement states that it was Herman House School and Kindergarten, run by a Mr. Kermode and a Miss Cassidy. A year later it was run by Miss Cassidy who was Irish, and Mr. Komoll, who was of German origin. The school was very popular with the wealthier residents of the area.

HERMAN HOUSE SCHOOL, c. 1913

This school group was photographed in the grounds of Herman House. The young lady, seventh from the left in the back row, was Edith Courvoisier. She was born on November 12th 1896; her mother was English and her father from Basel, Switzerland. Edith attended the school until she was eighteen and became a scholar of English, French and German and was also an accomplished solo singer and piano teacher. Her father died when she was eleven and she spent the next forty years caring for her mother. She never married and lived in Ravenswood Avenue for many years. She travelled extensively and gave many lectures on different subjects. After the death of her mother, Edith took up cycling and was a familiar figure riding her tricycle until a few years before her death in 1985.

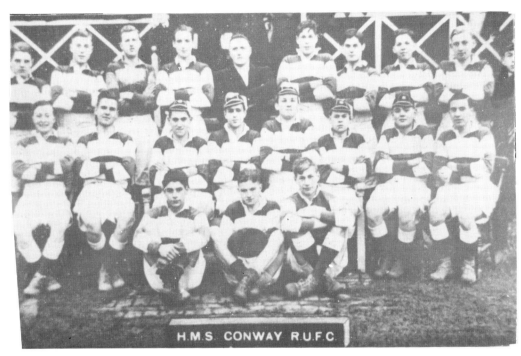

H.M.S. 'CONWAY,' R.U.F.C., c. 1936

The training ship owned a large sports pavilion and playing fields, which were used for cricket, football and rugby, situated in Knowsley Road. Inter-ship matches were also played here. The 'Conway' ran five rugby teams each season. From these teams came three international players, who all learned the game on these fields. The team, shown above, was photographed in front of the pavilion which was burnt down by vandals in 1972. Next to the fields there are now some high-rise flats and these stand on the site of the old H.M.S. 'Conway' hospital.

CHARLIE BROAD, c. 1921
Charlie was one of many coalmen who served Rock Ferry and supplied H.M.S. Conway with coal. He was the first to use motorised transport - in the form of a model T Ford.
He purchased this vehicle from a firm in Old Swan, Liverpool, who obtained them in kit form. Charlie had to collect the truck and drive it back after only fifteen minutes tuition from the salesman! A few days later he started to teach his father to drive and subsequently bought another vehicle for himself.
Here he is pictured with his horse "Silvo", at the corner of Acton Road, Rock Ferry. After his retirement, Charlie went to live with his daughter, Joyce, in Bebington.

DACRE HILL,
ROCK FERRY.

DACRE HILL, c. 1912

In the centre of the photograph is the shop which, from 1886, had been both a post office and a chemist's run by Henry Stanton. In 1897, Herbert White took over both businesses and it is his name that is over the shop in this picture. At this time, it was solely a chemist's as the post office had moved to new premises next door; the words "Dacre Hill Postal and Telegraph Office" can be seen between the trees on the right. In 1929, it was moved again to its present position on the opposite side of the road. The chemist's shop is still in business, now run by Mr. J. Carter. At the top of the hill, No. 54 was the home of Benedict Jones, local councillor and Freeman of the borough. In 1911, his house became the first telephone exchange.

GALTRES SCHOOL, DACRE HILL, c. 1910
The photograph was taken in the school grounds when it was in Dacre Hill. The group includes the Headmistress, the maid, the teacher and her pupils. The small boy, second from left in the back row, was Don Kemp. Later, the school moved to larger premises in Kings Lane, to a house previously owned by a Mrs. Casson. At the time, the headmistress was Mrs. Benson. Pupils at the school were easily recognised by the distinctive blazer badge, which was an owl. The building was pulled down in the late 1970s to make way for flats and town houses.

EGERTON PARK, c. 1910

The Park was first laid out in the 1860s. By 1874, only half-a-dozen houses had been built. In one of these lived Mr. George Atkin who was the "George" of George Henry Lee - the large Liverpool store. The Park was designed on similar lines to Rock Park with an oval road and houses on either side and in the middle. It also had a gated entrance at both ends. The large house in the centre of the picture still stands - unlike most of the Park. During World War 1, it was owned by a Doctor Noble who apparently employed maids and a footman - a necessity in such a large house. For many years now, the house has been used as a nursery school.

WOMEN UNIONISTS, EGERTON PARK, c. 1929
All dressed in their finery, the women pose for the photographer before setting off on
their day out to Llangollen. The ladies behind are already seated in the charabanc.

St Pauls Church, Rock Ferry.

ST. PAUL'S CHURCH, c. 1907
Although the church stands in
Rock Ferry, it was built to serve
the people of Tranmere.
The church was erected in 1855
with seating for 520 people. The
road leading to the church was
called Lime Kiln Lane but this
was thought to be too common a
name, so it was changed to
St. Paul's Road! The church has
changed little over the years and
is still a prominent feature of
Rock Ferry.

Kings Lane and Dacre Hill, Rock Ferry

DACRE HILL, c. 1903

This is the crossroads of Dacre Hill, Kings Lane and Old Chester Road, looking towards Dacre Hill. From this point, with only one or two houses in Kings Lane, the countryside began. Where the Kings Hotel now stands, there was once a wide stream where the children of the area used to play. In 1927 Benedict Jones wrote an article for the Birkenhead Advertiser entitled "Memories of an old Freeman" in which he states: "from the brook where we sailed boats in Kings Lane there was not the slightest suggestion that a town was near. It was as pure an agricultural district as could be found in England". Today, Fairs Cameras stands on the far left of the junction and Lloyds Bank is on the near right.

WOODBURN HOUSE, KINGS LANE, c. 1929
Built in the 1880s, Woodburn House was originally occupied by a Mr. David Allardyce, a
wealthy merchant. At the time, it backed onto a rough track through pine woodland -
this later became Kings Lane. When the house was built, the only other residence in the
vicinity was Larchwood House. This photograph was taken from a position that is now
Woodburn Boulevard. The house has been demolished and Lloyds Bank
stands on the site.

MR. AND MRS. ALLARDYCE, c. 1927

This delightful photograph was taken in the drawing-room of Woodburn House and shows Mr. and Mrs. Allardyce, who were very well-known and liked by the local people. A local resident, Mrs. Emily Beatty, remembers that every Christmas Day all the local people along with their children were invited to Woodburn House, where a party was laid on and everyone went home with a gift of some kind. Another resident, Jack Fairs, can remember being invited along with St. Paul's Sunday School and being given a bunch of sweet peas and an orange. Jack and his brother, Bill, have happy memories of the times they played in the woods behind the house.

49

KINGS LANE, c. 1912

Looking back towards Dacre Hill, this view could be a rural lane in the heart of the country. At one time it was used only by courting couples and occasional travellers. The author's mother could remember cows being herded down the lane to the dairy on Dacre Hill for milking. The gatehouse on the right was the entrance to Larchwood, a very large house set in its own walled grounds. It was owned by Mr. Thomas Hall, a merchant. The gateway is roughly where Kingswood Boulevard is today and on the left-hand side of the picture, behind the lamppost, is where Princes Boulevard now begins.

A "VULGAR" POSTCARD,
c. 1906

At the turn of the century, this type of postcard was considered to be very rude. Some church people did their best to have them banned from shops in Rock Ferry. This is another example of a stock card - the town's name has been added as appropriate. The phrase on the card was in common use at the time and was popularised by George Robey in one of his songs. Originally, it came from the old song "Knees up Mother Brown".

My word if I catch you bending
194   AT ROCK FERRY.

ENTRANCE TO THE DELL, NEW FERRY, c. 1902

These gates guarded the New Ferry entrance to Rock Park. The gate-keeper lived in Dell Cottage which was on the left behind the trees. The roadway led to a couple of houses and then on to Rock Park. In 1923, work commenced on the Dell Housing Estate and the gate-posts were removed prior to World War 2. Sadly, all the trees, Dean House and Dell House have now gone and have been replaced by modern houses and flats. The author remembers delivering newspapers here on many occasions as a small boy.

IN THE DELL, NEW FERRY, c. 1911

The Dell was frequented by Nathaniel Hawthorne on his regular evening walks around the district. In one of his letters he stated that he often heard a nightingale sing in the Dell which, at the time, was a beautiful wiend. Just inside the entrance to the Dell were the gates of Dean House - on the left of the picture. Unfortunately, they were destroyed during the blitz along with a neighbouring house.

THE GAP AND NEW FERRY PIER, c. 1906
On the left of the picture is the New Ferry end of the Esplanade which ran along the riverbank to Rock Ferry Pier. On the right is the pier with a ferry-boat and, in midstream, the sailing-ship is the 'Indefatigable' training ship. In the centre foreground some boys are playing at the river's edge in "The Gap".

THE GAP AND PROMENADE, NEW FERRY   No KNF4

THE GAP, NEW FERRY, c. 1920

Situated at the bottom end of the Dell, the Gap was a popular spot for children to play and paddle in the river. It was also used as a landing place by the boys of the "Akbar" and "Indie" when visiting their playing fields in New Ferry. In the summer months, Hope Hall of New Ferry held some of their Sunday School services here. Most of the service and singing was conducted by Dr. Greason of Rock Lane East.

The Pier from Hotel, New Ferry

NEW FERRY PIER, c. 1906

The pier was built of iron and opened to the public in 1865. Ferry rights were left to the Mersey Steam Boat Company which ran a triangular service between Liverpool Pierhead, Dingle and New Ferry. Birkenhead Corporation ran the ferry from 1897. Here, the ferry is seen in its heyday with many advertisements and vending machines outside the ticket office. In 1922, a steamer ran into the end of the pier destroying it. This prompted the closure of the ferry service and the pier was finally demolished in 1929, but part of the ticket office remained until after World War 2. This site is now a large car park and is frequented by birdwatchers and sightseers and is also a very popular spot with local people. In the picture, H.M.S. 'Indefatigable' can be seen to the left of the pier.

New Ferry Pier.

NEW FERRY FROM THE PIER, c. 1905

Looking back along part of the 850ft-long pier, there was a fine view of the New Ferry Hotel and New Ferry Terrace (The Esplanade). On the right of the picture is a large house that is believed to be Scott's Villa. Little is known about the building which has now gone, having sustained a direct hit during World War 2.

NEW FERRY ROAD, c. 1904

This row of fine shops with half-timbered frontages, once stood close to the pier.
Here one could purchase all manner of goods. From left to right the row comprised: the
Post Office, with a rack of postcards hanging from the doorway; a fishmongers;
a greengrocers; a tobacconist and a general store. Most of the shops had closed by the
late 1950s and were later converted to flats.

NEW FERRY SHORE, c. 1905

Once covered in golden sand, this part of the shore was known as Fisherman's Cove.
A number of rowing-boats were moored here. To reach the shore there was a pathway
leading down from the large houses at the bottom of Henthorn Road. When the author
was a boy, it was a place of great adventure. He can remember being chased along the
beach, past the privately owned Esplanade, after attempting to scale the high wall.
Today, the beach is heavily polluted and buried under tons of masonry - a far cry from
what it once was.

THE 'GREAT EASTERN', c. 1880
This famous ship, designed by Brunel, was brought to the area to be broken up. At first
she was moored at Tranmere and then moved to New Ferry. While here, the boys from
H.M.S. Conway boarded her, dismantled the stoves and kitchen fittings and then
transported them back to their own ship where they were fitted in the galley! Most of
the fittings were auctioned at a later date. Some doors and the bar can still be seen in
the Great Eastern Hotel today.

NEW FERRY BRICKWORKS, c. 1924

The photographer has captured the last moments of this stack and kiln during demolition at the brickworks. This works must have supplied most of the bricks with which Rock Ferry and New Ferry were built. It stood on a site known as Mayfields, on the shore of the River Mersey, where a clay pit was exploited almost as far as New Chester Road. Barges would come up the river during high tide, into a small, purpose-built dock, to be loaded with bricks for distribution as far afield as Northern Ireland. The site was later taken over by the council for use as a municipal tip and, today, it is used for football pitches.

THE 'CLARENCE', c. 1884

The 'Clarence' was the Catholic reformatory ship. She was an eighty-four gun liner battleship, launched in 1827. She began her role as a reformatory ship in 1864, with accommodation for 250 boys. In 1884, the ship came to a sad end when a few unruly boys set fire to her. The boys responsible were sentenced to five years penal servitude. In 1885, the 'Royal William' was renamed 'Clarence' and took up the post of reformatory ship but, in July 1889, she was set on fire and totally burnt out. The Bishop of Shrewsbury, along with some 235 boys and crew, was on board at the time but, fortunately, all were removed to safety. No further Catholic reformatory ships were moored in the Mersey.

OPEN AIR BATHS, NEW FERRY   No 4.

THE OPEN AIR BATHS, NEW FERRY, c. 1933

The swimming-baths were built in 1932 at a cost of £12,000. It catered for everyone, from young to old, swimmer and sunbather alike and had large grassed areas and trees. The pool itself was 330ft. long, 90ft. wide and had a water capacity of one million gallons. The water was drawn from the Mersey by a pumphouse, forced through filter beds and chemically treated. The depth of the pool ran from 3ft. to 16ft. and it had three slides, two springboards and fixed diving boards. The Baths were sold in the mid 1970s and filled in. A modern housing estate now stands on the site.

TRAM TERMINUS. NEW FERRY.

"The Unique Series".

THE TRAM TERMINUS, NEW CHESTER ROAD, c. 1904

The tram terminus was just to the right of the picture in New Ferry Road, now New Ferry Market. This crossroads had previously been the site of the old toll-bar which had always been a popular gathering place for local people. On the left of the picture, a large gas-lamp sits atop a signpost outside the Bank. The road to the left is Bebington Road and the signpost indicates that it is the way to Heswall and Neston. In the foreground, a delivery boy has just stepped off the right-hand pavement and appears to be making his way from Edge's Butchers shop, which is still trading under the same name today. The tram has reached the end of the line on New Chester Road - as can be seen by the absence of tram-lines or tram poles in the foreground.

THE OLD TOLL-BAR, NEW CHESTER ROAD, c. 1880

The stretch of New Chester Road from New Ferry to Bromborough was owned by
Mr. Birch of New Ferry who founded the toll-bar. He exacted payment from people
using his land as a thoroughfare. This practice lasted until 1872 when the tolls were
abolished. The toll-house, however, remained for several years but was eventually
abolished to make way for the North and South Wales Bank, now the Midland Bank.
On the left of the picture is New Chester Road and on the right is Bebington Road.

NEW CHESTER ROAD, c. 1915

This photograph was taken looking towards Bromborough from Boundary Road.
The road was opened in 1844, making New Ferry, formerly known as The Pasture, an
important stop-over for coaches and passengers on their way to Chester from
Birkenhead. There is very little traffic in this picture and the owner of a tricycle has
quite happily left it in the roadway. On the opposite side of the road, there is a post
office delivery-cart.

BEBINGTON ROAD, NEW FERRY, c. 1903

The photograph was taken looking back towards the site of the toll-bar. On the right, across New Chester Road, is Mr. Lacy's bakery where local people took their own dough to be made into bread. His slogan was "The cheapest and the best". Opposite is the black and white gable of the Wynnstay Hotel. On the corner of Bebington Road is Parr's Bank and adjacent to it is Davenport's clock shop, and a stationer's whose window is full of postcards. A sign reads: "High Class Postcards - Wholesale and Retail". These were probably printed by George Davies who had premises in New Chester Road, now occupied by C. J. Studios. This is one of his cards; how many more have survived - where are they now? On the left, Lloyds' newsagents has a Daily Post placard announcing a "Crisis in Persia".

TOWNFIELD LANE, BEBINGTON, c. 1911

In this view, looking towards Village Road, the two cottages are lavishly decorated with flags and bunting to celebrate the Coronation of King George V. The decorations have attracted the attention of some small girls who are climbing the railings for a better look! The building on the corner is the old Post Office and the large house across the road is Victoria Farm where, until the early sixties, there was a piggery which could be heard and smelt from some distance away! To the right of the farm is a footpath which runs through Mayer Park.

BEBINGTON POST OFFICE, THE VILLAGE, c. 1913

Before becoming a post office and general store, the building was an ale-house called the Dog and Gun. In 1886, it was run by a Mrs. Ann Deighton, beer seller, and in 1897 the licensee was Mr. James E. Green. The name can still be seen above the shop today although it is now a turf accountants. According to a local resident the post office was run by two spinster sisters in 1929 and the shop next door was run as a general store by their brother and his wife; their name was possibly Dodd. On the corner of Townfield Lane some local children are posing for the cameraman. One boy is wearing the uniform of a telegraph boy.

69

THE VILLAGE, BEBINGTON, c. 1907
The painted sign on the side wall of the Dog and Gun can be clearly seen on this
postcard. The sign also has the words: "Birkenhead Brewery Company's Celebrated
Ales". Outside the inn are two farm-carts, one of which has a load of hay. On the left
of the picture is the Wellington Hotel which was once a stopping point for the Bristol
mail-coach. On the right-hand side, the Bank was a branch of the North and
South Wales Bank and is now a local store.

WILLOW COTTAGE, THE VILLAGE, c. 1908

Locally known as "The Thatch", this cottage dates from 1656 when it was inhabited by Reginald and Annie Poole who farmed the surrounding land. At the time, the Grove was the main road past the house. However, in 1840, due to increased traffic and larger coaches pulled by six horses, Village Road was built as a straighter and safer route. As a result, what was originally the back of the house became the front. The cottage still stands today, looking much the same as it did all those years ago. If only it could speak!

"OLD BEBINGTON", c. 1913

This view of the Village is from Heath Road. The housewives from the terrace on the
left are only too pleased to take a break and pose for the photographer. On Village Road,
Ascroft's newsagents and greengrocers forms the centrepiece of the row of shops that
have long since been pulled down. The turrets and battlemented edging on the roofs are
the work of Thomas Francis. Convinced that Napoleon would win the Battle of
Waterloo, his idea was to mount wooden cannon in the turrets in the hope that it would
frighten away the French as they marched along Village Road after landing at
New Ferry!

BEBINGTON VILLAGE, c. 1909

A view of Bebington Village that shows the drinking fountain in the centre of the road.
Behind the group of boys at the fountain is Parr's Dairy and, just beyond, is Thomas
Francis' garden wall in which there are three stone slabs bearing "curious inscriptions".
These were later moved, together with the fountain, to Mayer Park. At the same time, all
the buildings on the left-hand side of the road, up to the Rose and Crown, were
demolished to make way for so-called "road improvements".

THE "CURIOUS INSCRIPTIONS", c. 1910

After a visit to Bebington, Nathaniel Hawthorne wrote: "In the village of Bebington we saw a house built in the imitation of a castle, with turrets in which an upper and lower row of cannon were mounted. On the walls there were eccentric inscriptions cut into slabs of stone, but I could not make sense of these". He thought it was the work of some crazy person but they were carved by the well-known eccentric Thomas Francis, a local stone-mason. Perhaps the most bizarre thing he did was to dig his own grave which he lined with stone. Each Saturday without fail, he visited his grave to brush it out and, when finished, would sit in it for hours, smoking. Francis died in 1850 aged 87. The stone on the right can be read by adjusting the spaces:- "A rubbing stone for asses".

MAYER PARK, BEBINGTON ROAD, c. 1906

The Park was originally a farm set amongst five acres of meadow and orchard. Joseph Mayer bought the site in 1861. The barn became Mayer Hall and the farmhouse became the Library. In 1864, the surrounding land became the Park. In those days walkers had an unobstructed view of Liverpool from the Park. The large granite boulders in the Park are, no doubt, erratics deposited by the last ice sheet some 100,000 years ago and originated from Scotland. Joseph Mayer was an admirer of Charles Dickens and named the main driveway after him.

MAYER HALL, BEBINGTON ROAD, c. 1905

Mayer Hall, the building with the tower, housed the library, built and opened by Joseph Mayer in January 1870. Stocked with ten thousand books, it proved so popular that people from all over the Wirral came to borrow books. It was decided to reduce its opening hours and restrict access just for the residents of Bebington. Joseph Mayer was born in 1803 and, for a short while, resided in Dacre Park, Rock Ferry. By 1864 he was living in Bebington in a house he renamed Pennant House, after a famous naturalist. He died in 1886 and was buried in St. Andrew's churchyard, a short distance from the lychgate. In the picture, the park gates are to the right of the Hall.

BEBINGTON ROAD, c. 1920

This part of Bebington has been transformed from the way it looked when the picture was taken. Of the two large houses on the right, 'The Orchards' still stands but 'The Poplars' has gone. The wall on the left has also gone and, on the extreme left, where there was once a fine bungalow, there is now a Gateway Superstore. Behind the trees, in the distance, was Bebington Hall and Council Offices. These are now the Planning and Rates Departments. The Rose and Crown can be seen in the distance with a few of the shops - the cross marks Marsh's shop.

NEW DRILL HALL. BEBINGTON. FOUNDATION STONE CEREMONY. 29/6/12.

NEW DRILL HALL, BEBINGTON, 29th June 1912
The foundation stone of Ormerod Hall was laid in June 1912, when boys of the Church Lads Brigade also laid stones, with their names on, near by. The drill hall stood in Bromborough Road, next to the church where there are now modern flats called Ormerod Court. By all accounts, Major Ormerod, after whom the buildings were named, was a very generous man. Born in Yorkshire in 1893, he moved to Bebington whilst still a young lad and became heavily involved with the Church Lads Brigade. He died in 1927 at the age of 54 and was buried in St. Andrew's churchyard. There were over 1,000 mourners at his funeral.

LOWER BEBINGTON SCHOOL, c. 1905

The original school was held in the belfry of St. Andrew's Church, but had to be moved to the priest's room or sacristy in 1720, due to lack of space. One can still see where some of the pupils carved their names, little realising that they were carving their own little piece of history. In 1828, Sir Thomas Stanley provided larger premises for a school in Acre Road. Then, in 1856, a piece of land was given to the Church for the purpose of building a new school; the benefactor being a Major J. C. Orred. In this photograph of the infant class, the girl, third from the left on the second row, is Margaret Valentine, neé Nagington, born 1897 and died 1965. She was the author's mother-in-law.

THE ROMAN ROAD. (OR KIRKET LANE.) BEBINGTON.

KIRKET LANE, c. 1905

At one time, this ancient walkway of Bebington was called Kirkgate Lane and then for many years was known as the Roman Road. It used to be paved with sandstone blocks and it is thought that the stone for the building of St. Andrew's Church was transported, from Storeton, along Kirket Lane. Apart from a short stretch into Cross Lane it has now gone completely.

MILL ROAD, NEAR BEBINGTON, c. 1909

The picture was taken a short distance from the school. For many years, the mill was a Higher Bebington landmark and stood proudly overlooking the Storeton quarries. It was built during the 1820s and was in use until c.1907, after which it was used as a store for farm machinery and soon became an attractive play area for local children.
It was originally owned by the Johnson family and later by the Williams family. The mill eventually became unsafe and was demolished in 1971.

Storeton Hill,
HIGHER BEBINGTON.

STORETON HILL, c. 1906

The hill is known locally as Rest Hill, which is the name supposedly given to the hill by the Romans who used it as a resting place whilst marching to Chester. The hill runs from Mount Road to Storeton village bisecting Storeton Woods. One of the Storeton quarries was situated to the right of the road and, inside, a piece of track and part of the original embankment can still be seen. A local resident, Mrs. Dora Boulton, tells the story of a gentleman who stopped at the Travellers Rest Inn, leaving his horse and trap unattended. Whilst inside, some local lads unhitched his horse while others took the trap and placed the shafts through the fence on the left of the picture. The horse was then rehitched leaving the trap on one side and the horse on the other!

STORETON WOOD, NEAR BIRKENHEAD.

STORETON WOODS, c. 1910

The picture shows the Great Cutting which was the entrance to the quarry. It is documented that one of the first owners was a Saxon by the name of Dunning. In 1086, it was owned by Nigel De Burcio. In 1282, after its deforestation by the Black Prince, it passed into the hands of the Stanley family. Today, it is owned by the Bowling brothers who purchased it in 1978 along with Storeton Hall Farm.

THE TUNNEL, STORETON QUARRIES.

T.S. B&C.

"The Unique Series."

THE TUNNEL, STORETON QUARRIES, c. 1906

The tunnel ran from Hancock's Wood, under Mount Road and through land owned by Mr. Norman Boulton. It was originally cut to cater for the Storeton tramway that carried large baulks of stone from the quarry. The tramway began in 1838 in the first quarry in Scotts Wood. The day that the tunnel opened, there was a party inside with some 200 workers in attendance. It is probable that a large quantity of home-brewed ale was drunk that day! Mrs. Dora Boulton remembers that the tunnel was used as an air-raid shelter during World War 2. She was quite happy in the tunnel until she noticed the cockroaches! The tunnel has now been filled in and very little evidence remains.

STORETON QUARRY, c. 1920

The two main quarries were situated on either side of Mount Road. The first to be extensively used was in the woodland to the right of Rest Hill. It is believed that the Romans may have worked this quarry. It was here, also, that the footprints of Cheirotherium were discovered in 1838 and subsequently, tracks of several reptiles were found eleswhere in the quarry. Many well-known local buildings are constructed of Storeton stone including St. Andrew's Church and Birkenhead Town Hall. The quarries were worked until the late 1940s and disused holes were used for the dumping of spoil from the two Mersey tunnels in 1934 and 1971. In the photograph, large baulks of stone can be seen to the left of the crane.

STORETON QUARRY COTTAGES, c. 1920
These were built in the early nineteenth century and were situated in the quarry itself close to Bracken Lane. The cottages were known locally as Gannie Johnsons and the surrounding wooded area was known as Jackie's wood. Mr. and Mrs. Johnson raised six children in the small cottages. Mrs. Dora Boulton's parents owned the land which remained unchanged until World War 2 when Birkenhead Council took over the quarries for dumping the piles of masonry from blitzed houses. They paid 1/- for each load to be dumped. Of the four cottages, only one stands today. The others had their roofs removed and were covered by tons of rubbish, but still stand about 6ft. below ground.

BRACKENWOOD HOUSE, c. 1929

The house was designed for the Evans family in the 1880s, by Sir Aston Webb, a brother-in-law of Mr. Evans. It was later sold to the Jacob family of the well-known biscuit-making firm. It came into Bebington Council ownership in the 1920s and was used as council offices with the large ballroom being used for wedding receptions. The gardens were impeccably maintained by a team of gardeners headed by Mr. J. Cliff. A nine-hole municipal golf course was laid out during the 1930s and was extended to eighteen holes some years later. Inside Brackenwood House a café and clubhouse were provided for golfers.

87

RABY MERE, c. 1907

The mere was a wonderful place with its cafe, rowing-boats, swingboats and those fabulous machines that were placed along the roadside: What the Butler Saw; Electric Shock Machine; Try your Strength; Bagatelle and the 1d. "ciggy" machine. All these have now gone but at least the crystal clear water where children played is still as clear today. The Williamson family has run the site since 1545 when it was probably started by Willmo Williamson, a gentleman of some wealth. In the photograph, the sign on the white building reads: "J. Williamson - Mill House - Tea Gardens". Today, the cottage behind the trees is owned by Mark Williamson.

DIBBINSDALE, c. 1931

This little bridge crosses the brook that runs through the Dibbin valley to the Mersey. The valley is the result of two or three glacial periods ranging from 10,000 to 4,000,000 years ago. Before the docks were built, the Mersey came up to this point and was used by small sailing-boats and barges transporting goods to and from the mill at Bromborough Pool. The shipping of goods ceased when the mill closed and the railway was built. The scene has changed little today, except for widening of the road and bridge.

SPITAL PARK, c. 1914
The park was once owned by Lord Brotherton and was later named after him.
The brook in the picture was once the home of otters. The children in the photograph
have been picking wild flowers. All the little girls have posies and their hats are
decorated with them. The park is now run by Wirral Borough Council as a nature
reserve and has two full-time rangers. The rustic bridge and brook are still there and the
park is a very popular place with both walkers and conservationists.